Inkwell Journeys: A Compellation of Prose

Faye Loughrey

BookLeaf Publishing

India | USA | UK

Inkwell Journeys: A Compellation of Prose
© 2023 Faye Loughrey

All rights reserved.

No part of this publication may be
reproduced, stored in a retrieval system, or
transmitted, in any form or by any means,
electronic, mechanical, photocopying,
recording or otherwise, without the prior
written permission of the presenters.

Faye Loughrey asserts the moral right to be
identified as author of this work.

Presentation by *BookLeaf Publishing*

Web: www.bookleafpub.com

E-mail: info@bookleafpub.com

ISBN: 9789358318272

First edition 2023

DEDICATION

To my daughter, your arrival showed me what unconditional love truly is.

ACKNOWLEDGEMENT

Without the encouragement of my family, this book would not exist.

42

The answer to life
Did not arrive as foretold
Though the towel's lovely

dreißig Juli
zweitausendsiebzehn

I still hold you Protective
Though I know you
Stopped being completely
Honest
Your words sweet in My ear
Starved of your melody
Until a word or phrase
Pings like a guitar string
Out of tune
But now I let you hold on to
Those lies
We both know you are telling
Because in the end
I've built scars around
Your betrayal
And you're still bleeding for Me

Gemini

Destined to be an enigma
always split between two worlds
Two sides of the same coin
love and madness swirled

You came in and calmed my soul
a bond that surprised more then you know
Feels like I've known you
another day from a long time ago

Took my hand
smoothed my edges with your voice
Unplanned
shut out all the noise

Always a duality
high and low
Spinning chaos in control
fast and slow

You are an ethereal light
beckoning all to draw near
Love in your own right
and still I fear

You chip away at my brick and mortar
through the Lath and Plaster
I've always been trouble and wonder
always a beautiful disaster

My darling friend
I've followed you down the rabbit hole
On a road I can't comprehend
out the window with self-control

Life is not the destination
learning through the journey
trial by ice and fire
calm seas, and winds gusty

And still I stand before the world
Pollux and Castor
Along for the trip
a little girl, dancer

Take my hand, hold my heart
stay near as I timidly travel
Following, watchful eye on the north star
as the path along starts to unravel

Love me through my back and forth
help me hold on
Watch me see through child-like eyes
the beginning of a new dawn

Tiny

5

The chair at my desk
Continues to slip down, down
I become tiny

Connected

Sky scraping trees tower over my head.
Loquacious birds fly from tree to tree
We arrive out here encircled by nature,
In the woods, where all is peaceful for me.

The muddy trails are soft
The fresh scent of greenery
The stillness of hiking mixed with
The cascading waterfall scenery

In a day, one could disappear.
Spiritually immersed with all near.
This is the chance to get away from it all
To let my mind and soul be free
Before again facing the everyday chaos
Alas, sadly a grown up reality.

Take my hand and trust my way,
I will show you the place I long to be.
The site we will one day slumber,
Take my hand and follow me.

Clutch my words, listen well
Release your heart too.
I will tell you of my stories
And keep close the history of you.

Sounds of water splashing against rocks
As it rages down streams
Traveling I know not where
Soothing sound puts my mind at ease.
I hear the resonance
Of the wind in the leaves
Crisp air, fresh, easy to breath
In this valley I have all I need

The butterflies arrive again
In my stomach and the meadow
The big grin returning to my face
The blush in my cheeks aglow
Your words, your thoughts
Filling a place in my head – my heart
Neglected for far too long
Excitement surrounding our start
The path of our friendship surrounded
By the path of these breathtaking trails
Enhanced by your presence, your philosophy
Intertwined, nature and intellect unveiled

Only a second was needed
To start this camaraderie
Under the tall trees, a quick flip of a coin
And the fates decide what the future may be
A ripple in the pond of life
New friendship, new spirit, new energy

So beautifully intricate
Gently testing the waters of our possibility
Sitting before a crackling fire
Soothing darkness wraps us in its arms.
With thousands of stars twinkling above,
Mother Nature's enchanting charms.
The future stretching onward
Kindred Spirit by my side
A life enhanced, forever changed
That you are in my life.

Thoughts Swirling

And the waiting becomes excruciating
I have done it again gone down the rabbit hole
of my mind… somersault after somersault until
The world is upside down
Excited about the possibility my mind goes on
full blast
Until the truth and the desired outcome become
tangled in
A web of desires and longing and wishes
mingling with the conversations of today and
yesterdays words play over and over each
syllable more delicious than the last
And a vulnerable honesty sent your direction
explaining the sensation of joy and of fear
Hopeful the words were clear enough, and not
childish or demanding
Lucid and light and inviting and then the doubt
whispers that I let my insecurities shine through
That I have made a fool of myself against all
that guarded exterior
You slipped through the side door reserved for
only a select few and sat yourself at the table as
if you had lived here for many years.
The easy going nature felt so right until I gave
myself a minute to think about it and realized

I left the smallest part of me in your hands
without knowing
Without a guarantee, without a word between
And now I sit and distract myself until I know If
that was the proper move a game of
Chess when we were only having tea
And will the trust be merited as I so suddenly
deemed it would
Climbing my way back to the day of light
Through the impossible insanity of the situation
And wishing for the crystal ball all the while
 And knowing that the unknown is the spice I
would sorely miss
I know I can only wait for you to answer the
question
I merrily sink back into my thoughts and play
the game of what if

E

My amazing child so quietly drifting asleep in
my lap.. always exploring.. Excited about the
things I have forgotten are exciting
A leaf….
The rainbows..
A loose tooth certainly to fall out tomorrow…
Or the next day…
and with that same wonder you devise solutions
to questions you haven't even asked.. and I
worry you are already too old to need your
momma..
Until you crawl into my arms asking to snuggle..
Just a moment longer.. Can I just sleep in your
bed tonight…
and I know I am blessed with so few of these
days.. you are an old soul.. Here to give the
world hope.. Those who know you cannot help
but to love you and I am your biggest fan
Do you remember when I was in your tummy
she says…
it was dark and I wanted to get out..
but it was warm and I wish I was still there…

Secretum

The conversations
Flow freely, secrets spoken
In my library

Brighter Than the Sun
inspired by Kadir Nelson's Heat Wave

Some days the sun beats down unwavering and
oppressive
Suffocating, windless day that even my plants
ensue submissive

And then there are days where my strength
outshines the sun
Reviving my potency, my tenacity, my grace, my
regal reach
The heat warming my tired frame and I extend
elegant
My upturned face rises to meet the rays of my
warm liege

My rich coffee skin glistening with diamond
beads
Presenting majestic out my city window
Too occupied to be troubled by my midnight
hound
Delighted in the coolness of my icy popsicle

Alice

The pain has come too quickly
This searing was to be joined with memory
So bittersweet it would move anyone
And now it is just bitter mixed with a trail of salt
My heart too afraid to beat
For fear that the water works will not end
The lump in my throat refusing to leave
The smile gone from the mouth that was always
upturned
With thoughts of you
Left only with a sudden panic
I guess this was too good to be true
Left running as the only option
If I am fast enough I can get in front of the pain
The sun wondering if it should stay away for another
day
Until the bleeding in my heart goes away
The sky falling from the clouds
And the rain forgot how to wash away this ache
You were the one that turned me upside down
And this lost Alice trying to find her way home
We find a connection like this once in a lifetime
If only we are lucky
And though you are not truly gone
I drown in the tears of my disapproval
To cause grief with the joy I freely give is more than I
can bear

Untitled

Run away with me
To the place where we are
Free from our responsibility
Lay by my side beneath the stars

Wrap your arms around
My shivering body
Until heartbeat is the only sound

Quiet the inner chaos
Sooth the doubt
Bring a smile across
The face without

Silence the screams
You will never hear
Even out the extremes

Look into my eyes
Peer behind the smile
The fear under here lies
Constant all the while

Little Girl

Little Girl you've found your way home
Through the nightmares and torture, you've left
untold
Little Girl you've found your way back
Though you were beaten, unloved, left off track
You rise through the ashes, take each burning step
Your soul has been cleansed by the tears that you
wept
And though your journey is far from done
You've turned your face out toward the sun
Each step you take brings strength to your heart
Each new friend you make, a shining new start
Welcome back to love, Little Girl, welcome back to
life
Welcome back to you, welcome back to the light
Each choice that you make to empower, to heal your
soul
These Angels encouraging the journey to make you
whole
Will keep leading you down this lighted path
Don't look around to the past aftermath
Keep looking forward to the future so bright
And always sing your love song each night
No longer fearing your future unknown
Welcome, Little Girl, you've found your way home

Untitled

You are the radiant sun, the light that graces the
start of each day.
You are the breath I yearn for, the exhale that
satisfies my deepest cravings.
You are my guiding moon in the night sky, a
beacon in my empty darkness.
You are the gentle whisper that shields me from
life's harshness.

If a flower were to possess a scent, it would
surely be your fragrance.
If a bird were to sing a song, your melody would
be its sweet resonance.
In a blossoming sunset, you'd be the vivid burst
of color.
You are the longing day that rescues me from the
relentless night.

I yearn for our trust to stand as unwavering as
ancient mountains.
The stars that adorn the sky are a testament to
your radiant light within the darkness.
You are the source of joy when tears fall, where
every moment holds significance.

You are my tranquil oasis, a calming breeze in
which I find reprieve.

If a child were to dance, your grace would guide
their steps.
If a hand were to offer care, it would be your
comfort they extend.
As tides sweep ashore, you are the compelling
current that draws me in.
And should a woman fall in love, you would be
the embodiment of the man.

Raindrops

19

Water dripping down
Are raindrops actually tears
Falling from heaven

Summer

In the embrace of the summer solstice
daylight stretches its golden wings
unveiling a world of enchantment
where time dances and dreams take flight
The solstice is a captivating moment
when the sun bathes us in an abundance
of radiant sunlight
a time when nature embraces the fullness of life
and the beauty of longer days unfolds before our
eyes
As the sun ascends to its highest point in the sky
a cascade of golden rays spills across the land
infusing everything with a vibrant glow
The world wakes
with renewed energy
as if nature itself
is celebrating the sun's triumphant reign
The extended daylight hours gift us
with a boundless canvas of time
inviting us to immerse ourselves
in the enchantment of summer
With the sun
lingering in the sky
painting it
with hues of

oranges
pinks
and purples
evenings become a symphony
of breathtaking sunsets
The horizon
transforms into a masterpiece
where the merging colors
seem to dance and blend
casting a spell of awe and wonder
Each sunset becomes a reminder
of the transient nature of life
urging us to cherish the fleeting moments
and find solace in their beauty
Fields adorned with
a kaleidoscope of wildflowers
sway gently in the warm breeze
their vibrant petals
reaching for the heavens
Forests come alive
with a chorus
of chirping birds
and buzzing insects
filling the air with a delightful melody
Majestic trees stand tall
their emerald leaves
providing a respite from the summer sun
while the murmurs
of babbling streams

and crashing waves
become an invitation
to seek solace in the embrace of water
The summer solstice serves
as a reminder of the Earth's graceful dance
around the sun
a celebration of
    light
    warmth
and the interconnectedness of all life
It invites us to savor the moments of joy
and to embrace the beauty that surrounds us

Slowly

I approach with a new cautious grace
Mindful of the steps I take
There is beauty in embracing the journey
Of getting to know him
And I relish the opportunity
To take this slow
Like a gentle waltz
I approach with an open heart
Yet guarded spirit
Recognizing the importance of
Patience
of
Allowing the connection to unfold naturally
With each interaction
I savor the moments
I appreciate the subtleties of his words
The nuances of his gestures
And the way his eyes
Reveal stories untold
I take pleasure in discovering
The layers of his being
Peeling back one at a time
Cherishing the anticipation
Of what lies beneath
As we embark on

This journey of discovery
I honor the importance of
Self care and self awareness
I listen to the whispers of my intuition
Acknowledging the boundaries
That protect my heart and well being
as well as his
Creating space to share fragments of
Our lives
Stories that reveal
Our triumphs, struggles, and dreams
Our conversations traversing
Both the lighthearted and the depths
Of our souls
In this deliberate slowness
We create a space to safely be ourselves
Free from judgement
Or pretense
We appreciate the quirks, Idiosyncrasies, and
imperfections
That make us beautifully human
For we are all interwoven through connection
We are of the stars

Chelan 23

In golden rays of the morning sun
Beneath the trees, their branches sway
A serene haven where relaxation is won
I lounge in bliss, letting time slip away
The sunbeams kiss my skin with warmth divine
Melting away stress, like sweet summer wine
A melodic conversation, with notes that amass
The piano keys tinkle, like raindrops on glass
The drums set the heartbeat, a pulsating groove
The singer croons, making feet move
The smooth saxophone whispers its tune
Painting emotions, like a tranquil moon
It dances with the bass, in syncopated delight
Creating a harmony that ignites the night
The air was adorned with melodic hues
Where the lake's serenity blends with the night
As nature's symphony gently pursued
In a realm where melodies take flight
And there amidst the enchanting space
We crossed paths, like rivers in the night
The waters shimmered in the moonlit embrace
Conversation so easily flowed
Where laughter danced and time took no pace
Each word a ripple, as our stories were bestowed
I stroll along pathways, kissed by golden rays

The scent of blooming flowers fills the air
A symphony of tranquility, a heavenly space
A fragrant serenade, beyond compare
In the stillness of mornings, I found inner peace
To witness nature's wonders, both great and
small
A chance to disconnect, to let worries release
Gratitude fills my heart, the greatest gift of all
I'm grateful for the journey, the places explored
For stepping outside my comfort zone's embrace
Open to discovering new horizons
And letting them leave a trace
I'm grateful for the laughter that filled the air
For shared adventures and stories untold
For the bonds strengthened, the friendships there
For one is silver, and the other gold

August 2020

Most nights I am ok, but then there are the ones
Where the darkness overcomes
Where the night terrors wake me screaming
Where my mind will not stop racing
Where sweet slumber is a dream
But I do not dream

The terrors are the only night time companions
and they leave my body shaking in a pool of
sweat
Undeserved
And not sweet like the sweat from a lovers
escapade
But cold
And chilling

I know there is no rescue
No one to save the day
    because the day passed
And it is night
But I can still feel the weight of him crushing
me
Smell his sickly sweet breath on the wind
Though decades later feel the cruel laughter that
fed me lies

And you said you would have rescued me
If only you had known
But you did not even try to talk to me
And even now you've grown
Into a man who says
"What did she do to provoke it"
And your hatred of so many
Flowing freely from your lips
And though I know it is yourself
You hate the most
You still do damage in your wake

And I feel like I am back there
Trying
Desperate to fit in
And I look into the mirror
Not knowing where to begin
Because as a kid when you learn
That people only call you
To make you the brunt of their new joke
You become an adult who believes
That every unread message
Is the proof of your
Automatic choke

And I wonder why the safety rules
Make my panic rise again
But the long term brush of cloth

Across my mouth
Reminds me of his brutal hands
And when they wrapped around my neck
Or when they covered half my face
And how he whispered
"Keep your mouth shut"
With a disappointed gaze

And while I lay here in the comfort of my home
As the demons of the past
Dance through my mind
    dance through my mind
        dance through my nightmares
I refuse sleep to find

And I can't stop this off key waltz
So I just sit in darkness
And count the seconds between
Each breath
Wondering if
The darkness will win
Or if tomorrow will bring relief

With the Right Framing

She is a collector of people
  and memories
Each lovingly placed on a desk
  on the wall
  on the shelf
Her eyes mist often in the night when she thinks
no one is watching
Though I watch
  waiting
For the moment she needs me
Carrying the weight of the world on her
shoulders - she knows no other way
  than to help
    help
      help
Contorting her body without the gracefulness of
a dancer
  she moves constantly
  quickly
Overwhelmed
The frustration sets in - the realization
  she cannot be in three places at once
Frame of reference skewed
  stolen innocence
Frame of mind skewed

always put on a happy face
She gazes at me - the photograph of her
grandmother resting in my solid bones
    gone 20 years ago today
    too soon
It is my time to shine
    I beam proudly in the sunlight
And gathers her strength to face another day
Sometimes, she catches a glimpse of herself
    reflecting in my glass
The image of her face and her grandmother blur
I see the spark come into her eye
    with the right framing she can handle anything

Mother

After the summer dry spell, petrichor was a
welcome scent
Each
          drop
                    falling
                              cleansing the earth
Weeping for the fire scorched land
Our mother's sadness
As we take..
          take…
                    take…
                              angry children fighting
for more
Meanwhile destroying the very life given to us
To go back to our roots
Deep
          below
                    underground
                              the womb of life
Earth providing
          the sweetgrass for calming and clearing
                    the summer strawberries for a
sweet burst of joy
And all we need is all around us when we stop to
listen

To the wisdom on the wind
To our mother's heartbeat
        consistent
            steady
                    even while slowly
breaking

Untitled

The book that caused all this
Was told and written by men with ego
And if they only stopped to embrace
The feminine wisdom
Bloodshed would have been from births not
deaths
He came to earth as a son
Because no one was listening to the Mother
But it was the women who he found were the
first
"Tellers of the good news"
And it was he who followed the feminine lead
Turn the other cheek
Acknowledged the daughter's of Abraham
Said there is more to a woman than bearing
children
And raising a husband
All are equal in the eyes
And since his departure
His truth has been lost
Manipulated
And twisted to fit the whims
Of egotistical men
Wealthy men
Who have mentally beaten women

Into a pigeon hole
Filled with Stockholm Syndrome and broken
dreams
You can only serve one Master
And they labeled their greed
God

www.ingramcontent.com/pod-product-compliance
Lightning Source LLC
Chambersburg PA
CBHW071234140726
47996CB00007B/2600